Isabella

Queen of Spain

Catherine Eden Brissette

PEARSON

Boston, Massachusetts
Chandler, Arizona
Glenview, Illinois
Upper Saddle River, New Jersey

Illustrations
Opener, 1, 2, 3, 5, 6, 7, 13, 14 Laszlo Verez.

Photographs
Every effort has been made to secure permission and provide appropriate credit for photographic material. The publisher deeply regrets any omission and pledges to correct errors called to its attention in subsequent editions.

Unless otherwise acknowledged, all photographs are the property of Pearson Education, Inc.

Photo locators denoted as follows: Top (T), Center (C), Bottom (B), Left (L), Right (R), Background (Bkgd)

4 Library of Congress; 8 Jupiterimages/Thinkstock; 9 Jupiterimages/Thinkstock, (Inset) Thinkstock; 15 Library of Congress.

ISBN-13: 978-0-328-67683-5
ISBN-10: 0-328-67683-7

16 17

Who Was Isabella?

One day in June 1491, a queen put on her suit of armor. She rode off to encourage her troops. This queen helped unite a divided land. She was no ordinary queen. Under her rule, Spain became a great **empire**.

Back then, queens were supposed to be quiet rulers. How did this queen—Isabella—become such a powerful leader?

Castile

On April 22, 1451, Isabella was born in Castile. Castile was a large kingdom in Europe. This region is where Spain and Portugal are now located.

Although Castile had a king, it lacked a strong central government. Wealthy **lords** had divided up Castile into smaller kingdoms. The lords and the king struggled for power.

The Kingdoms of Castile and Aragon, about 1450

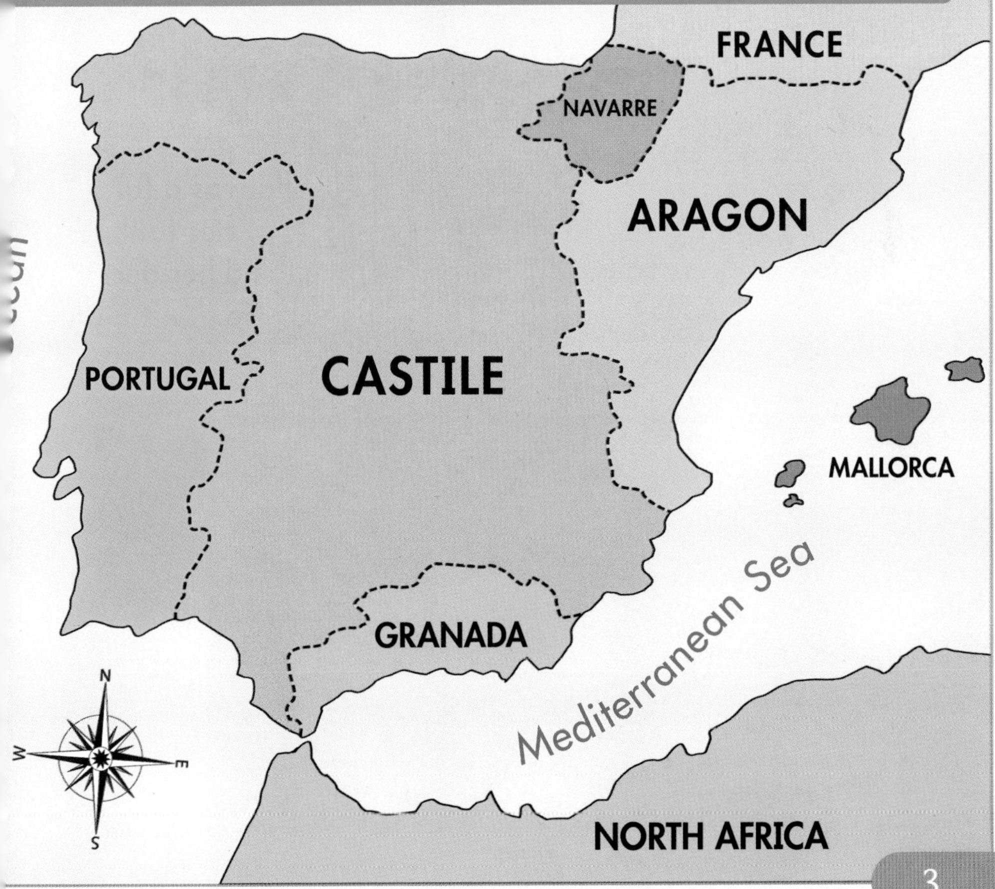

Preparing to Be Queen

Isabella's father died when she was three. Her older brother, Henry, became king. King Henry was afraid that his enemies would use Isabella to overthrow him. He forced Isabella to move to his court when she was thirteen. This way, he could keep a close watch on her.

Isabella did not like living in Henry's court. She did not know whom to trust there. She decided to trust herself and her Catholic faith.

Isabella was a faithful Catholic. Her faith influenced her decisions all her life.

The Marriage of Isabella and Ferdinand

Henry wanted Isabella to marry the king of Portugal. Henry had no son. He said that Isabella could be queen of Castile after he died, if she obeyed him.

Instead, Isabella decided to marry Ferdinand of Aragon. Like Castile, Aragon was a large Spanish kingdom. By marrying, Isabella and Ferdinand united two kingdoms into one country, Spain.

Who Is the Rightful Queen?

King Henry was angry that Isabella had ignored his wishes. He said that the future throne would not be Isabella's. Some people still supported Isabella as the next queen. Others did not.

After Henry died, this conflict resulted in a **civil war**. In the end, Isabella and Ferdinand's forces won. At last, Isabella was queen of Castile.

Spain was divided by civil war for four years.

Queen Isabella

After the war, Isabella worked to restore order in her kingdom. The civil war and King Henry's weak rule had caused problems in Castile. Isabella traveled many miles on horseback to help solve the problems people faced.

Isabella also raised her and Ferdinand's children. She certainly had her hands full! Yet, she wanted to do even more for her people.

The Conquest of Granada

Isabella and Ferdinand brought order to Castile. Next, they planned to **conquer** Granada. The Moors had ruled Granada for centuries. Moors were people of North African background who practiced Islam. By the end of 1491, Isabella and Ferdinand had captured nearly all of Granada. However, the capital city remained in the hands of the Moors.

The influence of the Moors can still be seen today in the many historic buildings of Granada.

Isabella and Ferdinand did not want to destroy the beautiful capital city. Instead, their army surrounded the city. After many months, the Moors ran out of food. Finally, they surrendered on January 2, 1492.

Isabella and Ferdinand decided that Spain must be a Catholic nation. They felt that this would keep Spain united. By 1492, they had ordered all Jews who had not become Catholic to leave Spain. Then, in 1502, they ordered all the Moors to become Catholic. If they did not, they also had to leave Spain.

Isabella and Ferdinand wanted to make Spain a Catholic nation. So the Inquisition, or official Church court, was set up to find out who was a "true" Catholic. As a result of the Inquisition, many Jews and Moors were jailed. Some were tortured and killed.

Isabella and Ferdinand met several times with Columbus before they agreed to support his first voyage.

The First Voyage of Columbus: 1492

After the conquest of Granada, a sailor named Christopher Columbus came to Ferdinand and Isabella. Columbus had an idea that would increase Spain's power even more. Columbus thought he could find a new trade route to Asia. He would sail west to Asia across the Atlantic Ocean. If he could reach Asia, the voyage would make him and those who helped him rich and powerful.

Advisors to Isabella and Ferdinand did not like Columbus's plan. They said that it was too costly and dangerous. But Columbus did not give up.

In the spring of 1492, Isabella and Ferdinand finally agreed to provide Columbus with ships and supplies. A successful voyage would make Spain richer and stronger. Isabella had another reason for helping Columbus. She planned to have the people that he met become Catholic.

In the late summer of 1492, Columbus and his crew left Spain. It was a long, difficult, and scary trip. Columbus's crew was afraid that they would die at sea.

Columbus sailed from Spain on August 3, 1492.

Spain Begins Building Its Empire

About ten weeks after they left Spain, the sailors found land. They thought it was an outer island of Japan. In fact, they had sailed to a Caribbean island.

Columbus explored for months. He claimed many islands for Spain. He believed that he had found islands near Asia. He named this region the West Indies. Columbus returned to Spain. He brought with him some gold, some plants, and people he called Indians.

When Columbus came ashore, he claimed the land for Spain. He did this even if people already lived there.

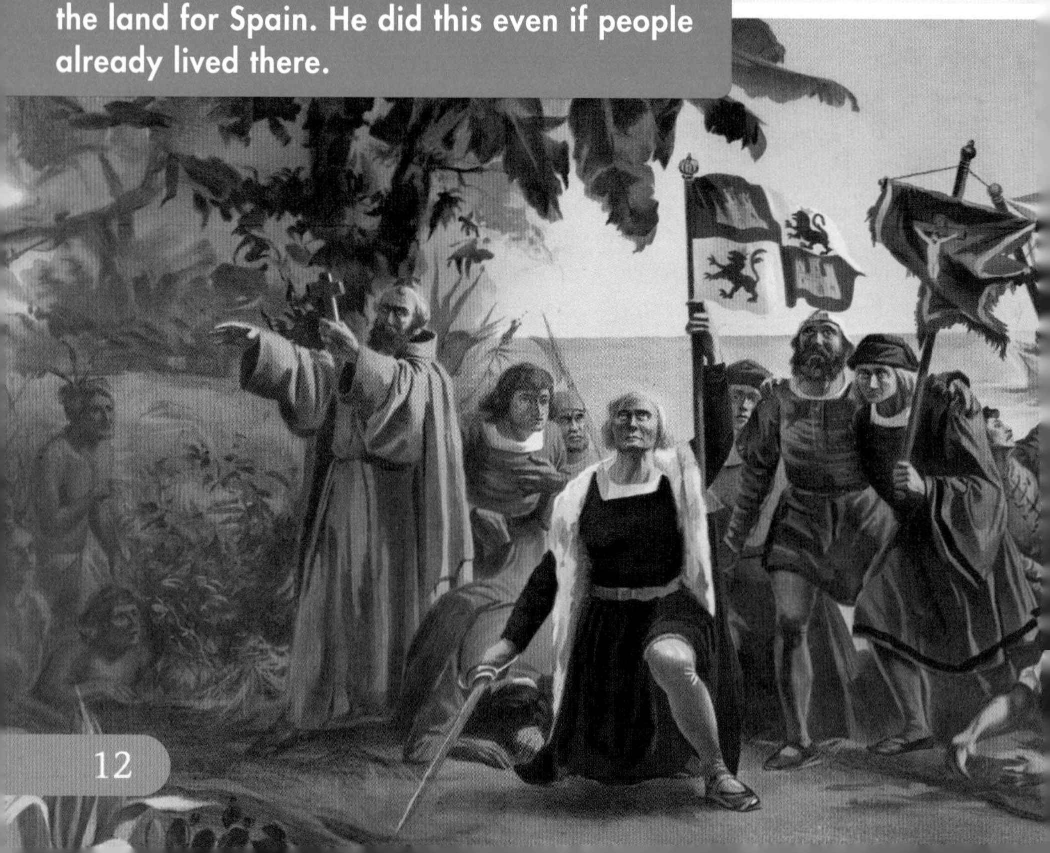

Columbus was a brave explorer and an excellent sailor. However, he wasn't very skilled at governing. He failed to stop some of his crew from mistreating the people of the islands.

Columbus was determined to bring back lots of gold. If he did not, his voyages would be seen as failures. He never discovered very much gold. Instead, he enslaved hundreds of people from the Caribbean islands. He brought them back to Spain and sold them as slaves.

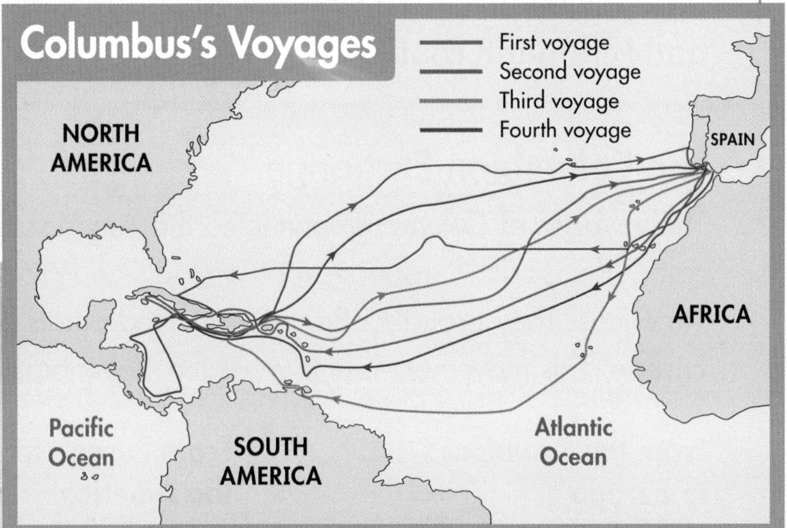

Isabella and Ferdinand sponsored Columbus on four separate trips across the Atlantic Ocean.

Isabella and Columbus

Isabella disliked how Columbus and his crew treated the people in the Americas. She expected Columbus to treat the people fairly. After all, she wanted them to become Catholic.

Isabella and Ferdinand were disappointed in Columbus. He didn't bring them back the riches they had expected. Still, Isabella knew that Columbus had brought honor and new lands to Spain. Now, Isabella and Ferdinand could make Spain into a world empire.

The Columbian Exchange

The voyages of Columbus connected the Americas to the rest of the world. Europeans took animals and plants to the Americas. They brought other animals and plants back to Europe. This movement is known as the Columbian Exchange.

From the Americas to Europe

turkeys 

chocolate 

tobacco 

corn 

potatoes 

From Europe to the Americas

cows 

horses 

pigs 

coffee 

sugar 

The Last Days of Queen Isabella

In 1504, Columbus returned from his last voyage. That same year, Isabella became very sick. Before she died, she asked that the people in the Americas be treated with respect. She still hoped that they would become Catholic.

Isabella had made many tough decisions. Her choices helped to unite Spain. In time, her united country became an empire. Today, the language and culture of Spain still influence people all around the world.

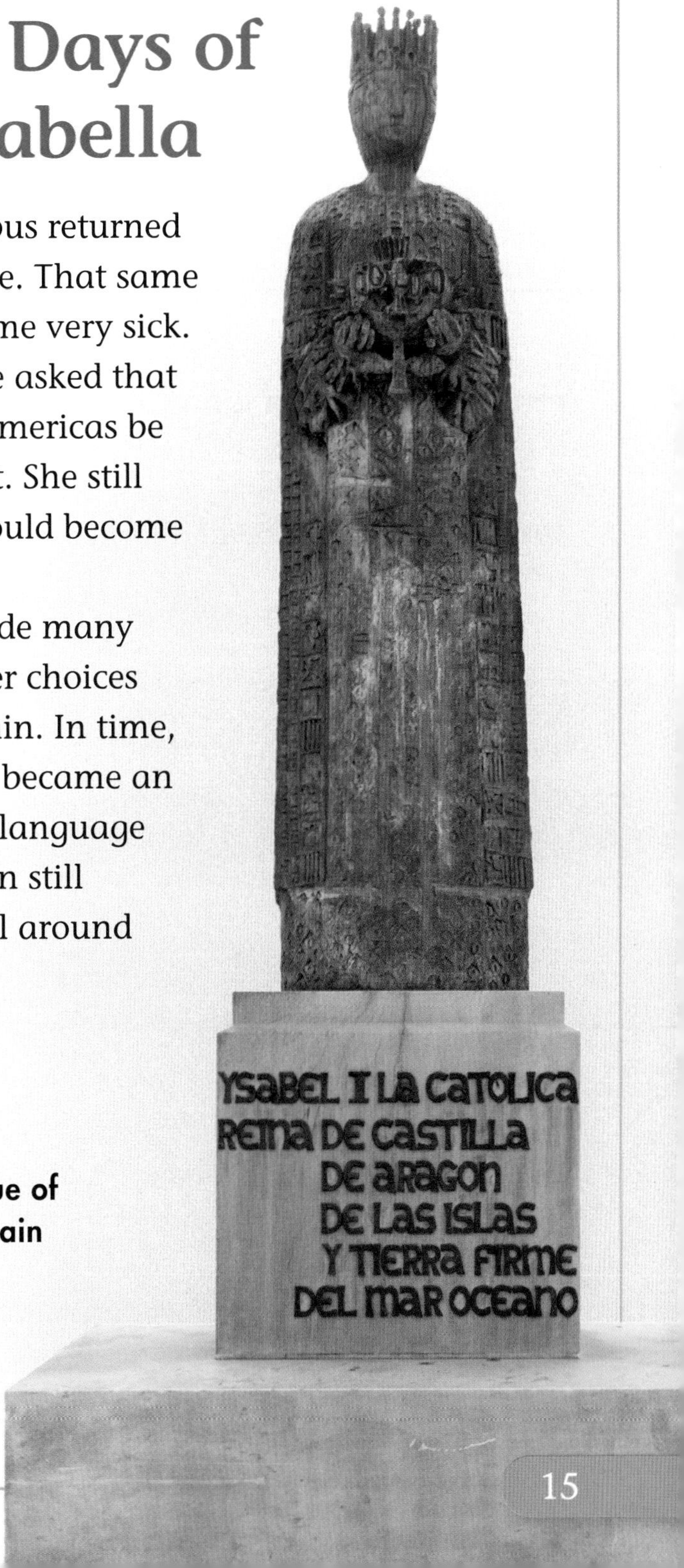

You can see this statue of Queen Isabella of Spain in Washington, D.C.

Glossary

civil war a conflict between two groups within the same country

conquer to defeat another country and take control of it

empire a group of lands and peoples ruled by one government

lord a noble who owned land and controlled it